book
Cocktails
and Mixed Drinks

BROCKHAMPTON PRESS
LONDON

© 1996 Geddes & Grosset Ltd, David Dale House,
New Lanark ML11 9DJ.

This edition published 1996 by Brockhampton Press,
a member of Hodder Headline PLC Group.

ISBN 0 86019 218 1

Printed and bound in the UK

CONTENTS

HISTORY OF THE COCKTAIL

Although the evidence proves that the idea of making mixed drinks existed centuries before the discovery of America, it is pretty well certain that the cocktail first became popular there.

In the 1920s, Prohibition banned the production and sale of strong liquor and to satisfy the 'underground' demand 'bootleg' spirits were manufactured and illegally distributed. These concoctions were often of very low quality and their frequently awful taste was best disguised by the addition of fruit juices, liqueurs and syrups. Following the repeal of the Prohibition laws in 1933 the fashion for mixing drinks continued to grow and spread across the Atlantic.

No one can say for certain where and how the term 'cocktail' originated, but there is a delightful story that first circulated during the American Wars of Independence. This tale features a New England tavern run by a Miss Betsy Flanagan which was often frequented by American officers. Near the tavern lived a prosperous landowner who was well known for his royal lifestyle and the officers frequently complained of his extravagances while they practically starved. One night Betsy served her customers a drink of rum mixed with fruit juice and decorated the concoction with a tail feather taken from the landowner's rooster. This became a very popular drink in the tavern and one night, in the midst of the revelry, a French officer called out 'Vive le coq's tail' as a toast.

Whether or not the story is true no one can say, but without a doubt, the sentiment expressed by the Frenchman has won wide acceptance around the world.

COCKTAILS AT HOME

Mixing

The most basic requirement of cocktail mixing is the
shaker. It is always better to have a shaker that also
contains a strainer as this will keep the ice separate from
the drink. When using the shaker, grip it with both hands
and shake vigorously—this is what makes a cocktail come
to life.

It is also important to have at hand a number of
teaspoons and tablespoons when mixing. These should be
kept in a glass of water and rinsed before and after use. A
perfectly good cocktail can be spoiled by the hint of
something that should not be in it.

Measures

It does not really matter what you use to measure the
ingredients of your cocktails. The important thing to
remember is that everything should be in the correct
proportion. In measuring quantities of spirits the term
'measure' refers to 45 ml (1½ fl oz), roughly 3 tablespoons. If you want to take a professional approach then
it is worth purchasing a standard measure, known as a
'jigger'. However, a measure can be anything you like—if
nothing else is available you can use an egg-cup or a
liqueur glass.

Serving
It is unlikely that you will have all the kinds of glasses normally used by cocktail barmen at your disposal. A good variety of glasses, however, makes things a lot easier—and more fun! Always chill glasses for at least 30 minutes before using them as cocktails should always be served as cold as possible.

Decoration
It could be said that some cocktails are not complete without the appropriate decoration. For example, some people would argue that a martini is not a martini without a stuffed olive. More often, decorations for cocktails, such as cocktail cherries and sprigs of mint, are a matter of personal taste. In this book some suggestions are made, but do not be afraid to experiment.

COCKTAIL RECIPES

In this section the ingredients of the recipes are given in proportional measures. Some cocktails, however, are topped up with soft-drinks or Champagne. How to make the 'base' for these drinks is therefore given proportionally, but the 'topping up' left to individual taste.

Stir and strain

Put ice into mixing glass, pour in the necessary ingredients, stir until cold, then strain into the required glass.

Shake and strain

Put ice into cocktail shaker, pour in the necessary ingredients and shake shortly and sharply unless otherwise instructed, then strain into the required glass.

Pour over ice

Half fill a tall glass with crushed ice and pour in the ingredients.

A

A.1.

⅓ Grand Marnier
⅔ dry gin
dash lemon juice
dash grenadine
Shake and strain.
Add a twist of lemon
peel.

ADONIS

⅓ sweet vermouth
⅔ dry sherry
dash orange bitters
Stir and strain.
Add a twist of orange
peel.

AFTER DINNER

½ brandy
½ cherry brandy
juice of ½ a lemon
Shake and strain.

ALEXANDER

⅓ brandy
⅓ crème de cacao
⅓ fresh cream
Shake and strain.
Sprinkle a little grated
nutmeg on top.

AMERICAN BEAUTY

¼ dry vermouth
¼ brandy
¼ orange juice
¼ grenadine
dash crème de menthe
Shake and strain.

AMERICANA

1 measure Bourbon
½ teaspoon castor sugar
dash Angostura bitters
Stir until sugar is dissolved
and top up with Champagne.

AMERICANO

2/3 sweet vermouth
1/3 Campari bitters
Pour over ice and top up
with soda water.
Add a twist of lemon
peel.

ANGEL FACE

1/3 gin
1/3 apricot brandy
1/3 Calvados
Shake and strain.

APPETIZER

1/2 gin
1/2 Dubonnet
juice of 1/2 orange
Shake and strain.
Decorate with a slice of
orange.

ASTORIA

2/3 gin
1/3 dry vermouth
dash of orange bitters
Shake and strain.

B

BACARDI

½ light rum
½ lime or lemon juice
1 teaspoon grenadine
Shake and strain.

BANANA BLISS

½ brandy
½ banana liqueur
Shake and strain.

BAMBOO

½ dry sherry
½ dry vermouth
dash orange bitters
Stir well and strain.
Add a twist of lemon
peel.

BARBICAN

1 measure Scotch whisky
dash Drambuie
2 dashes passion fruit juice
Shake and strain.

BENTLEY

½ applejack brandy
½ Dubonnet
Shake and strain.

BERMUDA ROSE

⅖ dry gin
⅕ apricot brandy
⅕ grenadine
⅕ lemon juice
Shake and strain.

BETWEEN-THE-SHEETS

⅓ brandy
⅓ dark rum
⅓ Cointreau
dash lemon juice
Shake and strain.

BLACK HAWK

½ Bourbon
½ sloe gin
Stir and strain.
Decorate with a cherry.

BLACK RUSSIAN

²/₃ vodka
¹/₃ Kahlua
Pour over ice.
(For a longer drink, use a
tall glass and top up with
Coca-Cola.)

BLACKTHORN

²/₃ sloe gin
¹/₃ sweet vermouth
dash orange bitters
Stir and strain.
Add a twist of lemon peel.

BLACK VELVET

¹/₂ Guinness
¹/₂ Babycham
Pour simultaneously into a
tall chilled glass.

BLOCK AND FALL

¹/₃ Cointreau
¹/₃ apricot brandy
¹/₆ anisette
¹/₆ applejack brandy
Shake and strain.

BLOODHOUND

¹/₂ dry gin
¹/₄ dry vermouth
¹/₄ sweet vermouth
2 or 3 fresh strawberries
Shake and strain.

BLOODY MARY

¹/₃ vodka
²/₃ tomato juice
3 dashes lemon juice
dash Worcestershire sauce
Shake and strain.
Add salt and pepper to
taste.

BLUE BOTTLE

¹/₂ dry gin
¹/₄ blue Curaçao
¹/₄ passion fruit juice
Stir and strain.

BLUE JACKET

¹/₂ dry gin
¹/₄ blue Curaçao
¹/₄ orange bitters
Shake and strain.

BLUE LADY

1/2 blue Curaçao
1/4 dry gin
1/4 lemon juice
dash egg white
Shake and strain.

BLUE RIBAND

2/5 gin
2/5 white Curaçao
1/5 blue Curaçao
Shake and strain.

BOBBY BURNS

1/2 Scotch whisky
1/2 sweet vermouth
3 dashes Benedictine
Shake and strain.
Add a twist of lemon
peel.

BOMBAY

1/2 brandy
1/4 dry vermouth
1/4 sweet vermouth
2 dashes Curaçao
Shake and strain.

BOSOM CARESSER

2/3 brandy
1/3 orange Curaçao
1/2 of 1 egg yolk
2 dashes grenadine
Shake and strain.

BOURBONELLA

1/2 Bourbon
1/4 dry vermouth
1/4 orange Curaçao
dash grenadine
Stir and strain.

BRAINSTORM

1 measure Irish whiskey
2 dashes dry vermouth
2 dashes Benedictine
Shake and strain.
Add a twist of orange
peel.

BRANDY (1)

1 measure brandy
2 dashes sweet vermouth
dash Angostura bitters
Stir and strain.

BRANDY (2)

1 measure brandy
2 dashes orange Curaçao
2 dashes Angostura bitters
Stir and strain.
Decorate with a cherry.

BRANDY EGG SOUR

1/2 brandy
1/2 orange Curaçao
2 dashes lemon juice
1/2 of 1 egg
1/2 teaspoon castor sugar
Shake and strain and pour
into a tumbler.

BRANDY FIX

2/3 brandy
1/3 cherry brandy
1 teaspoon sugar
1 teaspoon water
juice of 1/2 lemon
In a tumbler, dissolve the
sugar in the water.
Add crushed ice and the
remaining ingredients and
gently stir.

BRANDY FIZZ

1 measure brandy
3 dashes lemon juice
1/2 teaspoon castor sugar
Shake and strain and pour
into a tall glass.
Top up with soda water.

BRANDY FLIP

1 measure brandy
1/2 of 1 whole egg
3/4 teaspoon castor sugar
Shake and strain.
Sprinkle a little grated
nutmeg on top.

BRANDY GUMP

1 measure brandy
juice of 1 lemon
2 dashes greandine
Shake and strain.

BRAZIL

1/2 dry sherry
1/2 dry vermouth
dash Angostura bitters
Stir and strain.

BROKEN SPUR

2/3 port wine
1/6 dry gin
1/6 sweet vermouth
1 egg yolk
Shake and strain.

BROOKLYN

1/2 Bourbon
1/2 dry vermouth
dash maraschino
dash Amer Picon
Stir and strain.

BRONX

1/2 dry gin
1/6 dry vermouth
1/6 sweet vermouth
1/6 orange juice
Shake and strain.

BUCK'S FIZZ

1/4 orange juice
3/4 Champagne
Pour over ice in a tall glass.
Decorate with a slice of
orange.

C

Café de Paris

1 measure dry gin
1/2 of 1 egg white
3 dashes anisette
teaspoon fresh cream
Shake and strain.

California Dreaming

2/3 pineapple juice
1/3 Champagne
2 dashes Kirsch
dash lemon juice
Shake and strain pineapple
and lemon juice and Kirsch.
Pour into a wine glass and
add Champagne.
Decorate with a pineapple
ring.

Caruso

1/3 gin
1/3 dry vermouth
1/3 green crème de menthe
Shake and strain.

Casino

1/2 dry gin
1/4 lemon juice
1/4 maraschino
dash orange bitters
Shake and strain.
Decorate with a sprig of
mint.

Champagne

1 measure Champagne
1 sugar lump
dash Angostura bitters
Saturate the lump of sugar
with a dash of Angostura
bitters and crush.
Add ice and Champagne.

Champs-Elysées

3/5 brandy
1/5 Chartreuse
1/5 lemon juice
dash Angostura bitters
Shake and strain.

CHERRY BLOSSOM

1 measure cherry brandy
dash lemon juice
dash grenadine
dash Curaçao
Shake well and strain.

CHINESE

1 measure rum
dash Angostura bitters
3 dashes maraschino
1 teaspoonful grenadine
Shake well and strain.

CLARIDGE

$1/3$ dry gin
$1/3$ dry vermouth
$1/6$ Cointreau
$1/6$ apricot brandy
Stir and strain.

CLASSIC

$1/2$ brandy
$1/6$ lemon juice
$1/6$ Curaçao
$1/6$ maraschino
Shake and strain.

CLOVER CLUB

$2/3$ dry gin
$1/3$ grenadine
juice of $1/2$ lemon or 1 lime
$1/2$ of 1 egg white
Shake and strain.

CLUB

1 measure Bourbon
3 dashes grenadine
dash Angostura bitters
Stir and strain.
Add a twist of lemon peel.

COFFEE

$1/3$ brandy
$2/3$ port wine
2 dashes Curaçao
$1/2$ of 1 egg yolk
Shake and strain.

COMMODORE

$4/5$ Bourbon
$1/5$ lime juice
2 dashes orange bitters
Shake and strain.
Add sugar to taste.

CORCOVADO

1/3 tequila
1/3 Drambuie
1/3 blue Curaçao
Shake and strain and pour
into a tall glass.
Top up with lemonade.

CORONATION

1/2 sherry
1/2 dry vermouth
dash maraschino
2 dashes orange bitters
Stir and strain.

CORPSE REVIVER (1)

1/3 sweet vermouth
1/3 Calvados
1/3 brandy
Shake well and strain.

CORPSE REVIVER (2)

1/3 brandy
1/3 orange juice
1/3 lemon juice
2 dashes grenadine
Shake well and strain into a
tall glass.
Top up with soda water.

COWBOY

2/3 Scotch whisky
1/3 double cream
Shake and strain.

CUBA LIBRE

1 measure dark rum
juice of 1/2 lime
Pour over ice in a tall glass.
Top up with Coca-Cola.
Add a slice of lime.

D

DAIQUIRI

³/₄ dark rum
¹/₄ lime or lemon juice
¹/₂ teaspoon castor sugar
Shake and strain.
Decorate with a cherry.

DAIQUIRI BLOSSOM

¹/₂ orange juice
¹/₂ dark rum
dash maraschino
Shake and strain.

DANDY

¹/₂ Bourbon
¹/₂ Dubonnet
dash Angostura bitters
3 dashes Cointreau
Shake and strain.
Add a twist of orange or
lemon peel.

DEANSGATE

¹/₂ dark rum
¹/₄ lime juice
¹/₄ Drambuie
Stir and strain.
Add a twist of orange peel.

DEPTH CHARGE

¹/₂ brandy
¹/₂ Calvados
2 dashes grenadine
4 dashes lemon juice
Shake and strain.

DUBONNET ROYAL

²/₃ Dubonnet
¹/₃ dry gin
2 dashes Angostura bitters
2 dashes orange Cuaraçao
Stir and strain.
Decorate with a cherry.

E

EAST INDIA

³/₄ brandy
¹/₈ orange Curaçao
¹/₈ pineapple juice
dash Angostura bitters
Shake and strain.

EMPIRE GLORY

¹/₂ Bourbon
¹/₄ ginger wine
¹/₄ fresh lemon juice
2 dashes grenadine
Shake and strain.

EARTHQUAKE

¹/₃ gin
¹/₃ Scotch whisky
¹/₃ Pernod
Shake and strain.

EVANS

1 measure Bourbon
dash apricot brandy
dash orange Curaçao
Stir and strain.

F

FAIRY BELLE

3/4 dry gin
1/4 apricot brandy
1 egg white
1 teaspoon grenadine
Shake and strain.

FALLEN ANGEL

1 measure dry gin
juice of 1 lemon
2 dashes crème de
   menthe
dash Angostura bitters
Shake and strain.

FERNET

1/2 brandy
1/2 Fernet Branca
1 dash Angostura bitters
2 dashes Gomme syrup
Shake and strain.

FOURTH DEGREE

1/3 dry gin
1/3 dry vermouth
1/3 sweet vermouth
2 dashes Pernod
Stir and strain.

FRENCH 75

1 measure gin
juice of 1 lemon
1 teaspoon sugar
Shake and strain.
Top up with Champagne.

FROZEN DAIQUIRI

2/3 dark rum
1/3 lime or lemon juice
1/2 teaspoon sugar
dash maraschino
Shake well and serve
unstrained.

G

GIBSON

1/6 dry vermouth
5/6 dry gin
Stir and strain.
Add a' pearl onion.

GIMLET

2/3 dry gin
1/3 lime juice cordial
Shake and strain.

GIN COCKTAIL

1 measure gin
dash Angostura bitters
2 dashes orange bitters
Stir and strain.

GIN RICKEY

1 measure gin
juice of 1/2 lime or lemon
Pour over ice and stir.
Top up with soda water.
(Calvados, Bourbon,
brandy, rum or Scotch can
be substituted for gin.)

GIN FIZZ

1 measure gin
juice of 1/2 lemon
1 teaspoon castor sugar
Dissolve the sugar in
the lemon juice and add
the gin.
Shake and strain into a
tall glass.
Top up with soda water.

GIN SKIN

1/2 gin
1/2 lemon juice
3 dashes Gomme syrup
4 dashes strawberry syrup
Shake and strain.

GIN SLING

1 measure gin
1/2 teaspoon castor sugar
In a tall glass, dissolve the
sugar in water and add ice.
Pour in the gin and stir.
Top up with soda water.

GLOOM CHASER

1/4 Grand Marnier
1/4 orange Curaçao
1/4 grenadine
1/4 lemon juice
Shake and strain.

GOLDEN DAWN

1/4 dry gin
1/4 Calvados
1/4 apricot brandy
1/4 orange juice
Shake and strain.
Add a dash of grenadine.

GOLDEN FIZZ

1 measure gin
1/2 teaspoon castor sugar
3 dashes lemon juice
1 whole egg
Combine the gin, sugar and
lemon juice and stir to
dissolve the sugar.
Add the egg.
Shake well and strain into a
wine glass.
Top up with soda water.

GOLDEN GLEAM

1/2 brandy
1/2 Grand Marnier
dash lemon juice
Shake and strain into a
tall glass.
Top up with orange
juice.

GOLDEN HEATH

1/3 Drambuie
1/3 rum
1/3 sherry
Shake and strain.

GRAPEFRUIT

1/2 dry gin
1/2 grapefruit juice
dash Gomme syrup
Shake and strain.

GRASSHOPPER

1/3 white crème de cacao
1/3 green crème de menthe
1/3 double cream
Shake well and strain
into a wine glass.

GREENBRAIR

2/3 sherry
1/3 dry vermouth
dash peach bitters
Stir and strain.

GREEN ROOM

1/3 brandy
2/3 dry vermouth
2 dashes green Curaçao
Stir and strain.

GREEN DRAGON

1/2 dry gin
1/4 green crème de menthe
1/8 kummel
1/8 lemon juice
Shake and strain.

GRENADIER

1/2 brandy
1/2 ginger wine
dash ginger ale
1 teaspoonful castor sugar
Shake and strain.

H

HARVARD

½ brandy
½ sweet vermouth
2 dashes Angostura bitters
½ teaspoon castor sugar
Stir and strain.
Add a twist of lemon peel.

HARVEY WALLBANGER

⅕ vodka
⅘ orange juice
2 teaspoons Galliano
Pour the vodka and orange
juice over ice in a tall
glass.
Float the Galliano on top
using the back of a spoon.

HIBERNIAN SPECIAL

⅓ dry gin
⅓ Cointreau
⅓ green Curaçao
dash lemon juice
Shake and strain.

HONEYMOON

⅓ Benedictine
⅓ applejack brandy
⅓ lemon juice
3 dashes orange Curaçao
Shake and strain.

HORSE'S NECK

⅓ brandy
⅔ ginger ale
dash Angostura bitters
1 corkscrew cut lemon peel
Place the lemon peel in
the glass, securing it with a
cocktail stick at the top.
Add the bitters and ice.
Pour in brandy and ginger
ale.

HOULA HOULA

⅔ dry gin
⅓ orange juice
dash orange Curaçao
Shake and strain.

I

INK STREET
1/3 Bourbon
1/3 lemon juice
1/3 orange juice
Shake and strain.
Decorate with a slice of
orange or lemon.

INSPIRATION
1/4 dry gin
1/4 dry vermouth
1/4 Calvados
1/4 Grand Marnier
Stir and strain.

J

JACK-IN-THE-BOX
1/2 applejack brandy
1/2 pineapple juice
dash Angostura bitters
Shake and strain.

JACK ROSE
3/4 applejack brandy
1/4 grenadine
juice of 1/2 lime or 1 lemon
Shake and strain.

L

Leviathan

1/2 brandy
1/4 sweet vermouth
1/4 orange juice
Shake and strain.

Liberty

2/3 applejack brandy
1/2 Daiquiri rum
dash Gomme syrup
Shake and strain.

Light Rum Cocktail

1/2 light rum
1/4 lemon juice
1/4 grenadine
Shake and strain.

Little Devil

1/4 dry gin
1/4 dark rum
1/4 Cointreau
1/4 lemon juice
Shake and strain.

Little Princess

1/2 dark rum
1/2 sweet vermouth
Stir and strain.

London Fog

1/2 white crème de menthe
1/2 anisette
dash Angostura bitters
Shake and strain.

Los Angeles

1/2 Scotch whisky
1/2 lemon juice
1 fresh egg
dash sweet vermouth
Shake and strain.

Luigi

1/2 dry gin
1/2 dry vermouth
juice of 1/2 satsuma
1 teaspoon grenadine
Shake and strain.

M

MAGIC TRACE

$^4/_{10}$ Bourbon
$^3/_{10}$ Drambuie
$^1/_{10}$ dry vermouth
$^1/_{10}$ orange juice
$^1/_{10}$ lemon juice
Shake and strain.

MAGNOLIA

1 measure gin
$^1/_2$ teaspoon grenadine
1 egg white
juice of 1 lemon
dash of double cream
Shake and strain.

MAI-TAI

$^2/_3$ dark rum
$^1/_6$ apricot brandy
$^1/_6$ Curaçao
1 egg white
juice of $^1/_2$ lemon or lime
Shake and strain.

MAIDEN'S BLUSH

$^2/_3$ dry gin
$^1/_3$ lemon juice
1 dash Pernod
1 teaspoonful castor sugar
1 teaspoonful raspberry
  syrup
Shake and strain.
Decorate with a slice of
lemon.

MAIDEN'S PRAYER

$^3/_8$ gin
$^3/_8$ Cointreau
$^1/_8$ orange juice
$^1/_8$ lemon juice
Shake and strain.

MAINBRACE

$^1/_3$ Cointreau
$^1/_3$ gin
$^1/_3$ grapefruit juice
Shake and strain.

MANHATTAN

2/3 Bourbon
1/3 sweet vermouth
dash of Angostura bitters
Stir and strain.
Decorate with a cherry.

MANHATTAN (DRY)

2/3 Bourbon
1/3 dry vermouth
dash of Angostura bitters
Stir and strain.
Decorate with a green olive.

MANHATTAN (PERFECT)

2/3 Bourbon
1/6 dry vermouth
1/6 sweet vermouth
dash of Angostura bitters
Stir and strain.
Add a twist of lemon peel.

MAPLE LEAF

1 measure Bourbon whisky
juice of 1/2 lemon
1 teaspoonful maple syrup
Shake and strain.

MARGARET ROSE

1/4 gin
1/4 Calvados
1/4 Cointreau
1/4 lemon juice
dash grenadine
Shake and strain.

MARGARITA

1/2 tequila
1/4 Cointreau
1/4 lemon or lime juice
Shake and strain.
Before serving, moisten
the edge of the cocktail
glass, inside and out, with
lemon or lime and dip in
fine salt.

MARTINI

2/3 dry gin
1/3 dry vermouth
dash orange bitters
Shake and strain.
Decorate with a stuffed
olive or a twist of lemon
peel.

MARTINI (SWEET)

2/3 dry gin
1/3 sweet vermouth
dash orange bitters
Shake and strain.
Decorate with a cherry.

MARTINI (DRY)

2/3 gin
1/3 dry vermouth
Stir and strain.
Decorate with a stuffed
olive.

MARTINI (EXTRA DRY)

1 measure gin
dash dry vermouth
Stir and strain.
Decorate with a stuffed
olive.

MARY PICKFORD

1/2 dark rum
1/2 pineapple juice
1 teaspoon grenadine
dash maraschino
Shake and strain.

MAYFAIR

1/2 dry gin
1/2 orange juice
3 dashes of apricot syrup
Shake and strain.

MERRY WIDOW

1/2 sherry
1/2 sweet vermouth
Stir and strain.
Add a twist of lemon peel.

MILLIONAIRE

2/3 Bourbon
1/3 grenadine
1/2 of white of 1 egg
2 dashes orange Curaçao
Shake well and strain.

MILLION DOLLAR

2/3 dry gin
1/3 sweet vermouth
1/2 of white of 1 egg
1 teaspoonful grenadine
1 teaspoonful pineapple
juice
Shake well and strain.

MINT JULEP

1 measure Bourbon
1 sugar lump
1 teaspoon water
4–6 sprigs of mint
Crush the sprigs of mint,
sugar and water together in
a glass.
Add the Bourbon and fill
glass with ice.
Stir until glass is frosted.
Decorate with mint and
serve with straws.

MONKEY GLAND

1/3 dry gin
1/3 Pernod
1/3 grenadine
2 dashes orange juice
Shake and strain.

MONTANA

1/2 brandy
1/2 dry vermouth
dash port
dash Angostura bitters
dash anisette
Stir and strain.

MORNING GLORY

1/2 brandy
1/4 orange Curaçao
1/4 lemon juice
2 dashes Angostura bitters
Shake and strain.

MOSCOW MULE

1/5 vodka
4/5 ginger beer
Pour over ice in a long
glass.

N

NAPOLEON

1 measure dry gin
dash Dubonnet
dash Fernet Branca
dash Curaçao
Stir and strain.
Add a twist of lemon peel.

NEGRONI

1/3 dry gin
1/3 sweet vermouth
1/3 Campari bitters
Stir and strain.
Add a twist of lemon peel.

NEVADA

1 measure rum
juice of 1/2 grapefruit
juice of 1/2 lime
1 teaspoon Gomme syrup
Shake and strain.

NEW YORK

3/4 Bourbon
1/4 lime juice
2 dashes grenadine
1/2 tablespoon castor sugar
Shake and strain.
Add a twist of orange peel.

O

Old-Fashioned

1 measure Bourbon
dash Angostura bitters
1 sugar lump
teaspoon of water
Saturate the sugar lump with
the bitters and water.
Crush the sugar lump and
add whisky and ice.
Decorate with a slice of
orange.

Old Pal

1/3 Bourbon
1/3 dry vermouth
1/3 Campari bitters
Stir and strain.

One Exciting Night

1/4 gin
1/4 orange juice
1/4 dry vermouth
1/4 sweet vermouth
Stir and strain.

Opening Night

1/2 Bourbon
1/4 grenadine
1/4 sweet vermouth
Stir and strain.

Opera

2/3 dry gin
1/6 Dubonnet
1/6 maraschino
Stir and strain.
Add a twist of orange peel.

Orange Bloom

1/2 dry gin
1/4 Cointreau
1/4 sweet vermouth
Stir and strain.

Orange Blossom

1/2 gin
1/2 orange juice
Shake and strain.
Add a dash of grenadine.

P

PADDY'S NIGHT

1/2 Irish whiskey
1/2 green crème de menthe
Shake and strain into a
wine glass.
Top up with Champagne.

PALL MALL

1/3 dry gin
1/3 sweet vermouth
1/3 dry vermouth
1 teaspoon white crème
de menthe
2 dashes orange bitters
Shake and strain.

PARISIAN BLONDE

1/3 dark rum
1/3 double cream
1/3 orange Curaçao
1/3 teaspoon castor sugar
Shake well and strain.
Decorate with slices of
orange.

PERFECT LADY

1/2 gin
1/4 peach brandy
1/4 lemon juice
dash of egg white
Shake well and strain.

PINA COLADA

1 measure dark rum
1 tablespoon coconut milk
1 tablespoon crushed
pineapple
Shake well and strain into a
tall glass.
Serve with straws.

PINE VALLEY

1 measure gin
juice of 1 lime
1/2 of 1 egg white
1/2 teaspoon castor sugar
Shake and strain.
Decorate with several sprigs
of fresh mint.

PINK LADY

1 measure gin
1/2 white of 1 egg
1 tablespoon grenadine
Shake and strain.

PLANTERS

1/2 rum
1/2 orange juice
dash lemon juice
Shake and strain.

PLAZA

1/3 dry gin
1/3 sweet vermouth
1/3 dry vermouth
1 slice pineapple
Shake and strain.

PORT WINE

1 measure port wine
1 teaspoon brandy
Stir and strain.
Add a twist of orange peel.

PRESBYTERIAN

3/7 Bourbon whisky
2/7 ginger ale
2/7 soda water
Pour over ice and stir.
Add a twist of lemon peel.

PRINCESS MARY

1/3 dry gin
1/3 double cream
1/3 crème de cacao
Shake and strain.

R

RATTLESNAKE

$4/5$ Bourbon
$1/5$ lemon juice
dash egg white
dash Pernod
pinch castor sugar
Shake well and strain.

RED LION

$1/3$ dry gin
$1/3$ Grand Marnier
$1/6$ orange juice
$1/6$ lemon juice
Shake and strain.
Before serving, moisten
the edge of the cocktail glass
and dip in castor sugar.

REGENT STAR

$1/2$ dry gin
$1/4$ orange Curaçao
$1/8$ dry vermouth
$1/8$ passion fruit juice
Shake and strain.

RESOLUTE

$1/2$ dry gin
$1/4$ lemon juice
$1/4$ apricot brandy
Shake and strain.

ROADSTER

$1/3$ dry gin
$1/3$ Grand Marnier
$1/3$ orange juice
Shake and strain.

ROB ROY

$1/2$ Scotch whisky
$1/2$ sweet vermouth
dash Angostura bitters
Stir and strain.

ROOSEVELT

$1/4$ gin
$1/4$ rum
$1/4$ lemon juice
$1/4$ grenadine
Shake and strain.

ROSE

1/3 kirsch
2/3 dry vermouth
1 teaspoonful Framboise
Stir and strain.
Decorate with a cherry.

ROYAL

1/3 port
1/3 gin
1/3 Grand Marnier
dash Angostura bitters
Stir and strain.

ROYALIST

1/2 dry vermouth
1/4 Bourbon
1/4 Benedictine
dash peach bitters
Stir and strain.

ROYAL ROMANCE

1/2 gin
1/4 Grand Marnier
1/4 passion fruit
dash of grenadine
Shake and strain.

ROYAL SMILE

2/3 dry gin
1/3 Calvados
3 dashes grenadine
3 dashes lemon juice
Shake and strain.

ROYAL STANDARD

2/5 dry gin
2/5 apricot brandy
1/5 lemon barley water
Shake and strain.

RUSSELL HOUSE

1 measure Bourbon
dash orange bitters
dash Gomme syrup
2 dashes blackberry brandy
Shake and strain.

RUSTY NAIL

1/2 Scotch whisky
1/2 Drambuie
Pour whisky over ice in a
tumbler and float the
Drambuie on top using the
back of a spoon.

S

Salty Dog

4/7 vodka
3/7 grapefruit juice
pinch of castor sugar
Stir and strain.

San Francisco

1/3 sloe gin
1/3 sweet vermouth
1/3 dry vermouth
dash orange bitters
dash Angostura bitters
Stir and strain.

Sazerac

1 measure Bourbon
1/2 teaspoon castor sugar
dash Angostura
dash Pernod
Dissolve the sugar in the
Bourbon and add ice.
Stir and strain and add the
bitters and Pernod.
Add a twist of lemon peel.

Satan's Whiskers

1/5 dry gin
1/5 Grand Marnier
1/5 orange juice
1/5 dry vermouth
1/5 sweet vermouth
dash orange bitters
Shake and strain.

Scotch Mist

1 measure Scotch whisky
2 strips lemon peel
Squeeze the juice from the
lemon peel and add the
whisky.
Shake and strain.

Screwdriver

1/4 vodka
3/4 orange juice
Pour over ice in a tumbler
or long glass.
Decorate with a slice
of orange.

SEA FIZZ

1 measure Pernod
1 teaspoon sugar
juice of 1 lemon
Shake and strain.

SEVENTH HEAVEN

1/2 dry gin
1/2 Caperitif
dash Angostura bitters
2 dashes maraschino
Stir and strain.
Decorate with a cherry.

SHAMROCK

1/2 Irish whiskey
1/2 dry vermouth
2 dashes crème de menthe
2 dashes green Chartreuse
Stir and strain.

SHANGHAI

3/4 Jamaica rum
1/4 Pernod
2 dashes lemon juice
2 dashes grenadine
Shake and strain.

SHERRY TWIST

juice of 1 orange
3/4 sherry
1/4 Scotch whisky
2 dashes Cointreau
Shake and strain.

SIDECAR

1/2 brandy
1/4 Cointreau
1/4 lemon juice
Shake and strain.
Decorate with a slice of
lemon.

SILENT THIRD

1/3 Scotch whisky
1/3 lemon juice
1/3 Cointreau
Shake and strain.

SILVER FIZZ

1 measure gin
1 teaspoon sugar
juice of 1 lemon
1/2 of 1 egg white
Shake and strain.

SILVER JUBILEE

1/2 dry gin
1/4 banana liqueur
1/4 fresh cream
Shake and strain.

SINGAPORE SLING

1/2 gin
1/4 cherry brandy
1/4 lemon juice
Pour over ice in a tall glass
and top up with soda water.

SIX BELLS

1 measure dark rum
2 dashes orange Curaçao
2 dashes Angostura bitters
1 teaspoon castor sugar
juice of 1 lime
Shake and strain.

SNAKE-IN-THE-GRASS

1/4 gin
1/4 Cointreau
1/4 dry vermouth
1/4 lemon juice
Shake and strain.

SNOWBALL

1/4 Advocat
3/4 lemonade
Pour over ice.
Decorate with a slice of
lemon.

SPUTNIK

2/3 vodka
1/3 Fernet-Branca
1/2 teaspoon castor sugar
1 teaspoon lemon juice
Stir and strain.

ST GERMAIN

1 measure green Chartreuse
juice of 1/2 lemon
juice of 1/2 grapefruit
1 egg white
Shake and strain.

STAR

1/2 Calvados
1/2 dry gin
1 teaspoon grapefruit juice
dash sweet vermouth
Shake and strain.

STARBOARD LIGHT

1/2 dry gin
1/4 lemon juice
1/4 crème de menthe
Shake and strain.

STINGER

2/3 brandy
1/3 white crème de menthe
Shake and strain.

STRAITS SLING

1/2 gin
1/4 Benedictine
1/4 cherry brandy
juice of 1/2 lemon
2 dashes Angostura bitters
2 dashes orange bitters
Pour over ice in a tall
glass and top up with
soda water.

T

TANGO

1/2 dry gin
1/4 sweet vermouth
1/4 dry vermouth
2 dashes orange Curaçao
dash of orange juice
Shake and strain.

TEMPTATION

1 measure Bourbon
2 dashes orange Curaçao
2 dashes Pernod
2 dashes Dubonnet
1 piece orange peel
1 piece lemon peel
Shake and strain.

TEQUILA SUNRISE

1/4 tequila
3/4 orange juice
2 dashes grenadine
Shake and strain tequila and
orange juice.
Add grenadine.

TEMPTER

2/3 port wine
1/3 apricot liqueur
Stir and strain.

THIRD RAIL

1/3 Calvados
1/3 brandy
1/3 light rum
dash Pernod
Shake and strain.

THISTLE

1/2 Scotch whisky
1/2 sweet vermouth
dash Angostura bitters
Shake and strain.

THREE MILER

2/3 brandy
1/3 light rum
dash lemon juice
1 teaspoon grenadine
Shake and strain.

TOM COLLINS

1 measure gin
$1/2$ teaspoon castor sugar
juice of $1/2$ lemon
Shake and strain into a tall
glass.
Add ice and top up with
soda water.
(Rum, Calvados, brandy,
Bourbon, Scotch or vodka
can be used instead of gin.)

TRINITY

$1/3$ dry gin
$1/3$ sweet vermouth
$1/3$ dry vermouth
Stir and strain.

TWENTIETH CENTURY

$3/7$ dry gin
$2/7$ sweet vermouth
$2/7$ lemon juice
Stir and strain.

V

VANDERBILT

1/2 brandy
1/2 cherry brandy
2 dashes Angostura bitters
2 dashes Gomme syrup
Stir and strain.
Decorate with a cherry.

VALENCIA

1/3 orange juice
2/3 apricot brandy
4 dashes orange bitters
Shake and strain.

VIVA MARIA

2/3 tequila
1/3 lime juice
2 dashes maraschino
dash grenadine
1/2 of 1 egg white
Shake and strain.
Decorate with a cherry.

VODKA GIMLET

3/5 vodka
2/5 lime juice
1 teaspoon castor sugar
Shake and strain.
Decorate with a slice of
lemon or lime.

VODKA MARTINI

1/2 vodka
1/2 dry vermouth
Shake and strain.
Decorate with a twist of
lemon.

VOLGA BOATMAN

1/2 vodka
1/2 orange juice
1 teaspoon kirsch
Shake well and strain.
Decorate with a slice of
orange.

W

WARD EIGHT

2/3 Bourbon
1/3 orange juice
1 teaspoon grenadine
Shake and strain.

WEMBLEY

1/3 Scotch whisky
1/3 dry vermouth
1/3 pineapple juice
Shake and strain.

WESTERN ROSE

1/2 dry gin
1/4 apricot brandy
1/4 dry vermouth
dash lemon juice
Shake and strain.

WHISKY COCKTAIL

1 measure Scotch whisky
2 dashes Angostura bitters
2 dashes orange Curaçao
Shake and strain.

WHISKY FIX

1 measure Scotch whisky
1 teaspoon castor sugar
1 teaspoon water
juice of 1/2 lemon
Shake and strain.

WHISKY HIGHBALL

1/4 Scotch whisky
3/4 soda water or ginger ale
Pour over ice in a tall glass
and stir.

WHISKEY SOUR

3/4 Bourbon
1/4 lemon juice
1/2 teaspoon castor sugar
Shake and strain.

WHITE LADY

1/2 dry gin
1/4 lemon juice
1/4 Cointreau
Shake and strain.

WHITE LILY

$^1/_3$ Cointreau
$^1/_3$ rum
$^1/_3$ gin
Stir and strain.

WHITE ROSE

$^3/_4$ dry gin
$^1/_4$ maraschino
$^1/_2$ of 1 egg white
dash lemon juice
Shake and strain.

WHITE RUSSIAN

$^1/_2$ vodka
$^1/_4$ crème de cacao
$^1/_4$ double cream
Shake and strain.

WHITE SPIDER

$^2/_3$ vodka
$^1/_3$ white crème de menthe
Stir and strain.

– WHIZZ BANG

$^2/_3$ Scotch whisky
$^1/_3$ dry vermouth
2 dashes grenadine
2 dashes orange bitters
Shake and strain.

WIDOW'S KISS

$^1/_2$ Calvados
$^1/_4$ Chartreuse
$^1/_4$ Benedictine
dash Angostura bitters
Shake and strain.

X

XANTHIA

1/3 dry gin
1/3 Chartreuse
1/3 cherry brandy
Stir and strain.

X.Y.Z.

1/2 rum
1/4 Cointreau
1/4 lemon juice
Shake and strain.

Y

YELLOW DAISY

2/5 dry gin
2/5 dry vermouth
1/5 Grand Marnier
Stir and strain.

YELLOW PARROT

1/3 Pernod
1/3 yellow Chartreuse
1/3 apricot brandy
Stir and strain.

Z

ZAZA

1/2 dry gin
1/2 Dubonnet
dash Angostura bitters
Stir and strain.

ZAZARAC

1/3 Bourbon
1/6 light rum
1/6 anisette
1/6 Gomme syrup
dash Angostura bitters
dash orange bitters
2 dashes Pernod
Shake and strain.
Add a twist of lemon peel.

ZEUS

2/3 Campari bitters
1/3 vodka
Pour over ice and stir.
Add a twist of lemon peel.

ZOMBIE

1/3 dark rum
1/3 light rum
1/3 pineapple juice
2 dashes apricot brandy
2 dashes cherry brandy
1 teaspoon castor sugar
Shake and strain.
Decorate with pineapple
slices and a cherry.

WINE CUPS

BADMINTON CUP
TO SERVE 6 TO 8

1.5 litres (2½ pints) claret
30 cl (½ pint) sparkling
  mineral water
2 measures orange Curaçao
2 tablespoons castor sugar

Put the ingredients into a
large bowl or jug containing
plenty of ice. Stir gently.
Decorate with fresh fruit.

BALACLAVA
TO SERVE 6 TO 8

75 cl (1¼ pints) claret
30 cl (½ pint) sparkling
  mineral water
75 cl (1¼ pints) Champagne
juice of 1 lemon
1 tablespoon castor sugar

Mix the lemon juice with
the sugar in the bottom of a
large bowl. Add the other
ingredients and plenty of
ice. Stir gently. Decorate
with fresh fruit.

CHAMPAGNE CUP (1)
TO SERVE 4 TO 6

1.2 litres (2 pints) Champagne
2 measures brandy
1 teaspoon castor sugar
1 piece lemon peel

Mix the brandy with the
lemon peel and sugar. Add
Champagne and ice and
decorate with fresh fruit.

CHAMPAGNE CUP (2)
TO SERVE 4 TO 6

1.2 litres (2 pints) Champagne
2 measures brandy
2 measures orange Curaçao
1 measure maraschino
1 measure Grand marnier
1 tablespoon castor sugar

Put the ingredients into a large bowl or jug containing plenty of ice. Stir gently. Decorate with fresh fruit.

CIDER CUP (1)
TO SERVE 4 TO 6

1.2 litres (2 pints) cider
1 measure maraschino
1 measure orange Curaçao
1 measure brandy

Combine the ingredients in a large jug or bowl. Add ice and stir gently. Decorate with fresh fruit.

CIDER CUP (2)
TO SERVE 6 TO 8

1.2 litres (2 pints) cider
30 cl (1/2 pint) sparkling
   mineral water
2 measures sherry
2 measures brandy
juice and rind of 1/2 lemon
2 teaspoons castor sugar
pinch grated nutmeg

Combine all the ingredients in a large bowl. Add ice and stir gently. Decorate with fresh fruit.

CLARET CUP
TO SERVE 4 TO 6

1.2 litres (2 pints) claret

2 measures orange Curaçao

1 measure maraschino

2 tablespoons castor sugar

Combine the ingredients in a large jug or bowl. Add ice and stir gently. Decorate with fresh fruit.

PEACH CUP
TO SERVE 8 TO 10

1.5 litres (2½ pints) still Moselle, chilled

75 cl (1¼ pints) sparkling Moselle, chilled

3 tablespoons castor sugar

2 ripe peaches

Peel the peaches and place them in a large bowl. Add the still Moselle and the sugar; refrigerate for 1 hour. Add the sparkling Moselle just before serving. Do not add any ice to the drink.

MOSELLE CUP
TO SERVE 6 TO 8

1.5 litres (2½ pints) sparkling Moselle, chilled

2 measures brandy

30 cl (½ pint) sparkling mineral water

½ teaspoon maraschino

zest of 2 lemons

Combine all the ingredients in a large bowl. Stir very slowly—if you stir too rapidly the cup will lose its sparkle. Add ice before serving.

RHINE WINE CUP
TO SERVE 4 TO 6

1.2 litres (2 pints) white
  wine
1 measure orange Curaçao
2 measures maraschino
1½ teaspoons castor sugar

Combine all the ingredients
in a large bowl. Add ice
and decorate with fresh
fruit.

SANGRIA
TO SERVE 4

75 cl (1¼ pints) white wine
15 cl (¼ pint) cold water
10 tablespoons castor sugar
1 large lemon, thinly sliced
1 large orange, thinly sliced

Gently heat the sugar and
water in a small saucepan.
Add slices of fruit to the
syrup and leave to marinate
for 4 hours. Put ice, slices of
marinated fruit and syrup in
jug and add wine. Decorate
with fresh fruit.

PUNCHES

BRANDY PUNCH
TO SERVE 15 TO 20

2.25 litres (4 pints) brandy

2.25 litres (4 pints) sparkling
mineral water

30 cl (¹/₂ pint) orange
Curaçao

2 measures grenadine

juice of 12 lemons

juice of 4 oranges

625g (1¹/₄ lb) castor sugar

Dissolve the sugar in the
fruit juices. Transfer to large
bowl and add the rest of the
ingredients. Add ice and
decorate with fresh fruit.

BOMBAY PUNCH
TO SERVE 25 TO 30

1.2 litres (2 pints) brandy

1.2 litres (2 pints) sherry

4.5 litres (8 pints) Champagne

15 cl (¹/₄ pint) maraschino

15 cl (¹/₄ pint) orange
Curaçao

2.25 litres (4 pints) sparkling
mineral water

Combine all the ingredients
in a large bowl. Add ice
and decorate with fresh
fruit.

CARDINAL PUNCH
TO SERVE 25 TO 30

60 cl (1 pint) brandy
60 cl (1 pint) rum
60 cl (1 pint) sparkling white
  wine
2.25 litres (4 pints) claret
2.25 litres (4 pints) sparkling
  mineral water
2 measures red vermouth
500 g (1 lb) castor sugar

Dissolve the sugar in the mineral water. Transfer to a large bowl and add the rest of the ingredients. Add ice and stir slowly. Decorate with fresh fruit.

FISH HOUSE PUNCH
TO SERVE 12 TO 15

30 cl (1/2 pint) brandy
15 cl (1/4 pint) dark rum, or
  substitute a lighter rum
  like Bacardi
15 cl (1/4 pint) peach brandy
1.75 litres (3 pints) sparkling
  mineral water
juice of 6 lemons
250 g (8 oz) castor sugar

Dissolve the sugar in the lemon juice. Transfer to a large bowl and add the rest of the ingredients. Add ice and decorate with lemon slices before serving.

ROMAN PUNCH
TO SERVE 15 TO 20

1.2 litres (2 pints) Champagne
1.2 litres (2 pints) dark rum
1/2 measure orange bitters
10 egg whites, beaten
1 kg castor sugar
juice of 3 oranges
juice of 10 lemons

Dissolve the sugar in the fruit juices. Add the rest of the ingredients. Add ice and decorate with orange slices before serving.

SAUTERNES PUNCH
TO SERVE 10 TO 15

2.25 litres (4 pints) Sauternes
1 measure maraschino
1 measure Grand Marnier
1 measure orange Curaçao
250 g (8 oz) castor sugar
1/2 pint of fruit (hulled strawberries, peeled peaches or orange segments)

Place the fruits of your choice in a jug or bowl. Add the maraschino, Curaçao and Grand Marnier and refrigerate for 1 hour. Add plenty of ice and pour in the wine. Stir slowly and decorate with fresh fruit.

EGG-NOGS

CLASSIC EGG-NOG
TO SERVE 1

1 measure dark rum
1½ measures Scotch whisky
15 cl (¼ pint) milk
1 whole egg
1¼ teaspoons castor sugar
pinch of ground nutmeg
1 strip lemon peel

Combine the whole egg with the sugar in a mixing glass. Add the spirits and milk and transfer mixture to a shaker. Shake and strain. Sprinkle nutmeg on top and add a twist of lemon peel.

HOLIDAY EGG-NOG
TO SERVE 12

75 cl (1¼ pints) Scotch whisky
30 cl (½ pint) dark rum
45 cl (¾ pint) milk
1 litre (1 ¾ pints) cold double cream
10 eggs, whites and yolks separated
7 tablespoons castor sugar
grated rind of 1 orange
grated rind of 1 lemon
pinch of ground nutmeg

Beat the egg whites with 5 tablespoons of castor sugar in a bowl. Beat the egg yolks separately. Place the cream and the rest of the sugar in the punch bowl and beat until thick. Slowly pour in the egg mixtures, beating constantly, and then the spirits and milk. Sprinkle on nutmeg and the rinds. Chill before serving.

HOT DRINKS

CAFÉ BRÛLÉ
TO SERVE 4 TO 6

6 measures Cognac
60 cl (1 pint) hot coffee
6 strips lemon peel
6 small pieces of cinnamon
tablespoon of castor sugar

Moisten the rims of the glasses with the lemon and dip in the sugar. Put cinnamon and lemon peel in the glasses. Warm the Cognac, pour it into the glasses and set aflame. Let it burn out before adding the coffee.

CAFÉ BRÛLOT
TO SERVE 4 TO 6

3 measures brandy
1 measure Curaçao
60 cl (1 pint) strong black coffee
1 piece cinnamon
6 whole cloves
1 orange rind, cut into thin slivers
1 lemon rind, cut into thin slivers
3 lumps of sugar

In a small bowl or chafing dish, mash the sugar, rinds, cloves and cinnamon together. Add the brandy and the Curaçao and stir the mixture. Step back and ignite the brandy. Gradually add the coffee until the flame is extinguished.

GROG

TO SERVE 1

2 measures dark rum
15 cl (1/4 pint) boiling water
1 small piece cinnamon stick
1 slice lemon studded with
  2 cloves
1 teaspoon castor sugar

Place the lemon, sugar and cinnamon in a glass. Add the rum and stir to dissolve the sugar. Pour in the boiling water. Stir and serve.

HOT BUTTERED RUM

TO SERVE 1

2 measures dark rum
30 cl (1/2 pint) hot milk
1 small piece cinnamon
1 1/4 teaspoons castor sugar
1 tablespoon unsalted butter
pinch of ground nutmeg

Place the sugar, cinnamon and rum in a mug and stir to dissolve the sugar. Pour in the hot milk and add the butter. Sprinkle nutmeg on top before serving.

HOT TODDY

TO SERVE 1

2 measures Scotch whisky
15 cl (1/4 pint) boiling water
1 strip lemon peel stuck with
  1 clove
pinch of castor sugar
1 small piece cinnamon stick

Place the ingredients in a warmed glass or mug. Top up with boiling water. Stir and serve immediately.

IRISH COFFEE
TO SERVE 2

15 cl (¼ pint) Irish whiskey

45 cl (¾ pint) strong hot coffee

4 strips orange peel, each studded with 2 cloves

4 strips lemon peel, each studded with 2 cloves

1 stick cinnamon

2 scant teaspoons castor sugar

3 tablespoons whipped double cream

Gently heat the clove-studded peels in a frying pan with the sugar and cinnamon. When the sugar has melted add the whiskey. Stand back and set aflame. Shake the pan gently until the flame dies out. Pour in the hot coffee and simmer. Remove from the heat and serve. Top each serving with a dollop of whipped cream.

QUICK IRISH COFFEE
TO SERVE 1

1 measure Irish whiskey

15 cl (¼ pint) strong hot coffee

1 scant teaspoon sugar

1 tablespoon whipped double cream

Place the sugar in a warmed glass and add the whiskey and then the coffee. Stir to dissolve the sugar, and top with a dollop of whipped cream.

Non-Alcoholic Drinks

Anita

1/2 orange juice
1/2 lemon juice
3 dashes Angostura
    bitters
Shake and strain into a tall
glass.
Top up with soda water.

Cinderella

1/3 orange juice
1/3 lemon juice
1/3 pineapple juice
dash grenadine
Shake and strain into a tall
glass.
Top up with soda water.

Clayton's Pussyfoot

1 measure Coca-Cola
2 dashes lemon syrup
2 dashes orange syrup
Shake and strain into a tall
glass.

Jersey Lily

1 measure sparkling apple
    juice
2 dashes Angostura bitters
1/4 teaspoon castor sugar
Stir and strain into a wine
glass.

Keelplate

2/3 tomato juice
1/3 clam juice
2 dashes Worcestershire
    sauce
pinch of salt
Shake and strain.

Lemonade

juice of 1 lemon
1 1/2 teaspoons sugar
Half fill tall glass with ice.
Stir slowly and fill up with
plain water.
Decorate with a slice of
lemon.

LIMEY

2/3 lime juice
1/3 lemon juice
1/2 of 1 egg white
Shake and strain into a
cocktail glass.

NON-ALCOHOLIC EGG-NOG

1 measure milk
1 egg
1 teaspoon sugar
Shake well.
Grate a little nutmeg on top.

NURSERY FIZZ

1/2 orange juice
1/2 ginger ale
Pour over ice.

ORANGEADE

juice of 1 orange
1 teaspoon sugar
Half fill tall glass with ice.
Stir and fill up with plain
water.
Decorate with a slice of
orange.

PARSON'S SPECIAL

1 measure orange juice
4 dashes grenadine
1 egg yolk
Shake and strain
Add a dash of soda water

PUSSYFOOT

1/3 orange juice
1/3 lemon juice
1/3 lime juice
dash of grenadine
1 egg yolk
Shake and strain.

RASPBERRY LEMONADE

Same as Lemonade, but
add 2 dashes of raspberry
syrup.

ST CLEMENT'S

1/2 orange juice
1/2 bitter lemon
Shake and strain into a tall
glass.
Decorate with a slice of
orange.

SAN FRANCISCO

1/4 orange juice
1/4 lemon juice
1/4 pineappe juice
1/4 grapefruit juice
2 dashes grenadine
1 egg white
Shake and strain into a
wine glass.

STRAWBERRY LEMONADE

Same as Lemonade, but
add 2 dashes of strawberry
syrup.

SWEET AND SOUR

3/5 lime cordial
2/5 double cream
1 teaspoon honey
2 dashes Angostura bitters
Shake well and strain into a
cocktail glass.

TOMATO JUICE

1 measure tomato juice
2 dashes Worcestershire sauce
2 dashes salt
Shake and strain into a tall
glass.